COATS OF ARMS

ANDREW STEWART JAMIESON

From the dawn of civilization, people have adopted and used symbols to explain their existence, beliefs and culture. It was a natural progression to develop a system of symbols that both identified individuals and represented their place in society. This system is called heraldry. It evolved during the 12th century and is a rich cultural tapestry of lions, unicorns and other symbols. It tells of kings, knights and damsels, love, loyalty, honour and pride, and has inspired artists, writers and craftsmen for generations.

As we begin the new millennium, heraldry still flourishes because of its ability to absorb the new, link it with the past and provide continuity with the present.

The Beginning of heraldry

↗ *A battle scene from the Maciejowski Bible (c.1250) showing the carnage and confusion of a medieval battlefield.*

↗ *Coats of arms could only be devised by the official heralds. Early heralds were fond of devising arms for heroic characters from antiquity. This is one of several coats of arms designed for King Arthur.*

DURING THE MIDDLE AGES, armour became increasingly sophisticated and the medieval warrior found himself encased in iron from head to toe, with a closed helmet which rendered him anonymous. The medieval battlefield was a dangerous place, where it was essential to know who were your friends and who were your enemies: marks of identity that were easy to recognize in the heat of battle were clearly needed.

The shield was the main defence. It presented a broad flat surface, ideal for showing an adopted symbol or pattern, called a charge. The use of the charge was extended, so that very quickly it could be seen on the surcoat, a garment which covered the armour and gave protection from sun and rain, and from which we get the term 'coat of arms'. The horse caparison (a cloth which covered the horse) and ornaments, banners and flags and personal seals also showed the owner's charge.

Charges were adopted as insignia. At a time when most people could not read, seals were often the only means of 'signing' a document, and they provide some of the most beautiful examples of early medieval heraldry.

A good example of an → *equestrian seal from the 13th or 14th century. It shows a fully armed and mounted knight.*

Enamel plate from the tomb of Geoffrey → *Plantagenet, Count of Anjou and Maine who died in 1151. This is the earliest known surviving example of coloured heraldry, showing a blue shield with its gold 'lioncels'.*

· THE CROSS AND THE SWORD ·

The Crusades lasted from 1071 to 1291. European kings led Christian armies to fight the Muslims for control of Jerusalem and the Holy Land (Palestine). The cross was adopted as the primary symbol of the Christian forces, though its colour differed according to the wearer's country of origin.

The cross was also used on the arms of the great religious orders fighting in the Holy Land. The knights of each order could be identified by the shape and colour of the cross they displayed on their shields and wore on their mantles, over their surcoats.

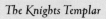

The Knights Templar

The Knights of St John

The Knights of St Lazarus

The Teutonic Knights

↖ *The arms of the four main religious orders. These troops were disciplined soldiers who had taken religious vows – corps of fighting monks at the centre of the Christian forces.*

Heralds

THE FIRST HERALDS were probably wandering minstrels whose ability to memorize the great heroic songs of love and war made them well suited for remembering and recounting the devices on the shields that they saw on their travels all over Europe. Their skills of recognition were employed in battle to identify the arms and banners of opposing forces.

By the late 14th century, heralds held a prominent position within the court or household. Heralds were also called officers of arms and were organized by the marshal. In peacetime the heralds compiled armorial records and organized tournaments.

Tournaments began as a brutal sport, but by the 14th and 15th centuries they had developed into a highly organized series of ceremonies and pageants closely bound up with heraldic display. Under the control of the heralds, strict codes of conduct and behaviour were enforced on and off the 'field of honour'. To break this code, or to act in any way unchivalrously, could bring dishonour to a knight,

and, more importantly, to his coat of arms – the very symbol of his family name and pride.

One important ceremony was the 'helm show', in which knights would present their helmet and crest to the heralds or judges and the ladies of the court. The ladies would name those knights who they felt were tarnished in some way and the unfortunate knight would have his helm identified by the herald and cast to the ground.

As the tournament grew more elaborate a 'theme' would be announced and the heralds would sometimes devise special arms or pictorial references for use during the festivities. Such events gave the herald ample opportunity to show off his skill.

↓ *This colourful scene was painted by King René of Anjou to illustrate his famous manuscript 'Le Livre du Tournois'. It shows the high heraldic tradition of the medieval tournament in which knights fought for the honour of chivalry and their lady.*

← An early medieval shield of arms belonging to William the Marshal, Earl of Pembroke, who during the late 12th and early 13th centuries was considered by many of his age to be the 'Prince of the Tournament and the Flower of Chivalry'.

← A parade shield from the late 15th century. Instead of the usual heraldic device, the shield shows a painted scene on the theme 'Vous ou la Morte' (You or Death).

Illuminated initial from → a 15th-century grant of arms showing a medieval officer of arms.

• THE COLLEGE OF ARMS •

Today the heralds, or officers of arms, are members of the Royal Household and work from Her Majesty's College of Arms, which was founded by King Richard III. The College is made up of the Kings of Arms, Heralds and Pursuivants, working from their chambers. Their function is to assign and grant coats of arms, organize and participate in great ceremonies of state, and conserve and record heraldic and genealogical records.

The coat of arms of → Her Majesty's College of Arms.

5

AT THE END of the Hundred Years' War in 1453, large numbers of lesser gentry and yeomanry returned from France and were employed in the 'private' armies of wealthy families, such as Neville and Percy. They wore the livery (colours) and badge of the family and provided military service in return for the family's protection.

By the late 15th century, developments in arms and armour left little room for personal heraldic display. During the Wars of the Roses, soldiers (often foreign mercenaries) fought beneath a knight's standard or colours. At Bosworth in 1485, for example, some soldiers wore the green and white jackets of troops loyal to the Earl of Richmond, others the red jackets of the troops fighting for Sir William Stanley, and so forth. These soldiers also wore the personal badge of their commander in the field: they were in effect professional soldiers wearing uniform.

↗ *The wearing of badges was popular throughout the Middle Ages. In this detail from the Wilton Diptych, painted for King Richard II, the angels wear Richard's badge of a white hart.*

↓ *A variation of the firesteel badge of the dukes of Burgundy taken from a company standard captured during the Swiss Wars of 1475–77.*

↗ *Badges are still granted by the officers of arms. Th . recent example gra . .to Stephen Screech.*

← A standard belonging to Thomas Howard from the Wars of the Roses (15th century).

The arms of Louis of Bruges → are an example of 15th-century Anglo-Burgundian heraldry. The arms in the centre were given to him by King Edward IV of England when he appointed Louis Earl of Winchester for services to the House of York.

← Although not a strictly heraldic rendition, the artist of this wonderful border illumination hinted at the unrest of his time by showing a boar (the symbol of the Yorkist king Richard III) sniffing a red rose (the symbol of the house of Lancaster).

• TO ALL AND SINGULAR! •

The grant of arms is an illuminated document on vellum which assigns a coat of arms to an individual and his heirs. During the Middle Ages it was seen as an act of ennoblement, and the arms assigned would show a virtue in the bearer or would set a great example for future generations of the family to emulate. Some coats of arms alluded to the bearer's name, for example, trumpets for Trumpington or hirondelles (swallows) for Arundel. Grants of arms are issued today to individuals, companies, charities, academic and professional associations and institutions on condition that certain criteria are met.

← A grant of arms dated 1477 to Thomas Barowe in recognition for his clerical services to the Duke of Gloucester.

The language of heraldry

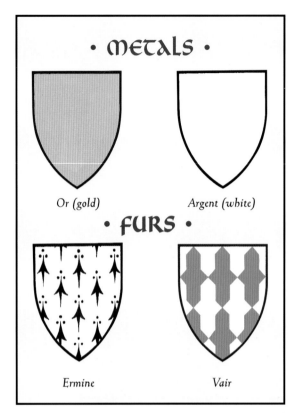

· METALS ·

Or (gold)   Argent (white)

· FURS ·

Ermine   Vair

BLAZON is an heraldic language adopted by early heralds to regulate and control the use of colours, charges, and so on. This language was originally in French and Latin and still uses words from these languages. Blazon totally and precisely describes a coat of arms in such a way that there is no room for doubt or confusion.

The coat of arms is centred on a shield, its most important component. There are five colours which are called tinctures. There are also two metals and several furs. Gold (Or) can be depicted as yellow and silver (Argent) is depicted as white. The most common furs are Ermine and Vair (grey squirrel). Rules were developed whereby tincture was never placed over tincture or metal over metal.

The surface of the shield is known as the field and the art of good heraldry is to keep the field as simple as possible, using as few tinctures, metals, shapes and objects as possible.

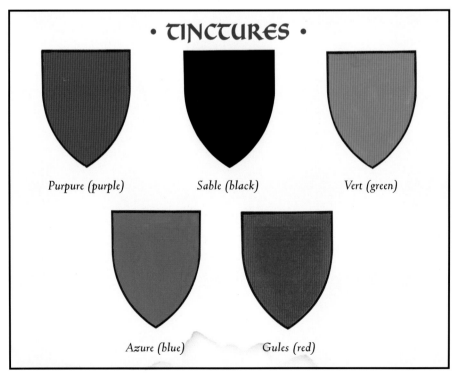

· TINCTURES ·

Purpure (purple)   Sable (black)   Vert (green)

Azure (blue)   Gules (red)

· ORDINARIES ·

Simple geometric shapes placed on the shield are known as Ordinaries. They have been used since early heraldry.

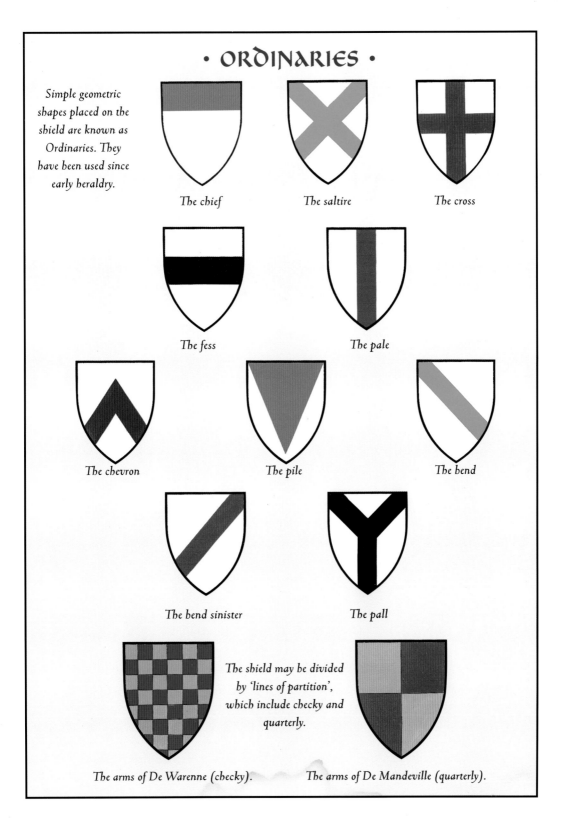

The chief

The saltire

The cross

The fess

The pale

The chevron

The pile

The bend

The bend sinister

The pall

The shield may be divided by 'lines of partition', which include checky and quarterly.

The arms of De Warenne (checky).

The arms of De Mandeville (quarterly).

Charges & Helmets

SHAPES AND OBJECTS PLACED on the shield are called charges. Some charges feature military subjects, such as scaling ladders, arrows or other weapons. A complete heraldic bestiary evolved with fantastic creatures based on classical mythology and the herald's imagination. Charges such as lions were given different terms to show their 'attitude' – Guardant (looking at you), Dormant (lying down), Rampant (standing on one back leg), and so on.

In more recent times, symbols of contemporary civilization have begun to appear on coats of arms: the symbol of the atom and an heraldic representation of the internet are two examples.

The charges – which include Ordinaries – and colours can be placed and combined on the shield in an infinite variety as shown in these examples.

↗ Some arms are blazoned counter-changed, as in the case of Geoffrey Chaucer, whose coat of arms is described as Per Pale Argent and Gules a Bend Counterchanged.

Arms that show a → *charge repeated many times are called 'Semé'. The Royal Arms of France show Semé de lis (fleur-de-lis repeated).*

← Drops shown on a shield are termed 'Gouttée'. These are Gouttée d'or.

↗ The arms of Mowbray: Gules a Lion Rampant Argent.

↗ The arms of Monthermer: Or an Eagle Displayed Vert armed (beak and claws) and langued (tongue) Gules.

↗ The arms of Hawkwood: Argent on a Chevron Sable three Escallop shells of the Field (i.e. the same tincture as the shield) Argent.

↗ The arms of Hastings: Argent a Maunch (lady's sleeve) Sable.

↗ The arms of Sidney: Or a Pheon (arrowhead) Azure.

↗ The arms of Shakespeare: Or on a Bend Sable a Spear of the first (i.e. first mentioned metal) the point steeled proper.

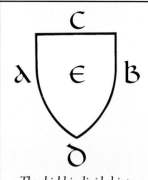

The shield is divided into various sections or points, the main ones being:

A. *Dexter side*
B. *Sinister side*
C. *Chief*
D. *Base*
E. *Fess point*

↗ *The arms of Hugh Le Despenser, Lord Le Despenser, Earl of Winchester, who died in 1326.*

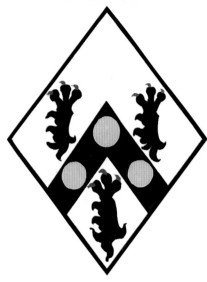

↗ *The arms of Jane Austen. A woman has traditionally used her father's arms on a diamond-shaped shield called a lozenge.*

The sovereign and royal princes

A peer of the realm

Baronets and knights

Esquires and gentlemen

· HELMETS ·

Helmets (helms) have appeared in coats of arms in many guises depending on the fashion of the time. During the Middle Ages little regard was given to style or colour and it is only in more recent times that rules have been issued as to which helm should be used by whom.

Blazoning a Coat of Arms

BLAZONING is the heraldic term for describing a coat of arms. First the field (background) of the shield is described, then the principal charge, followed by lesser charges on the field and lesser charges on the principal charge. A full coat of arms (in heraldry the correct term is an Achievement of Arms) usually includes the shield, the crest and a helmet of rank. A motto often appears but in England it is not strictly necessary. In certain cases, for example peers of the realm and senior knights, the shield may be held by figures, animals or fabulous beasts, and these are called supporters.

The coat of arms shown below is that of Peter Henry Greenhill, Gentleman of the County of Dorset. It is blazoned thus: Per chevron Gules and Vert three oval Buckles two and one their double tongues upward Argent and for the Crest upon a Helm with a Wreath, Argent, Gules and Vert between two Grassy Hillocks proper a Garb Or banded of a Strap Gules garnished with a buckle double tongued Argent Mantled Gules and Vert doubled Argent. The blazon therefore builds a step by step picture of the coat of arms, as shown opposite.

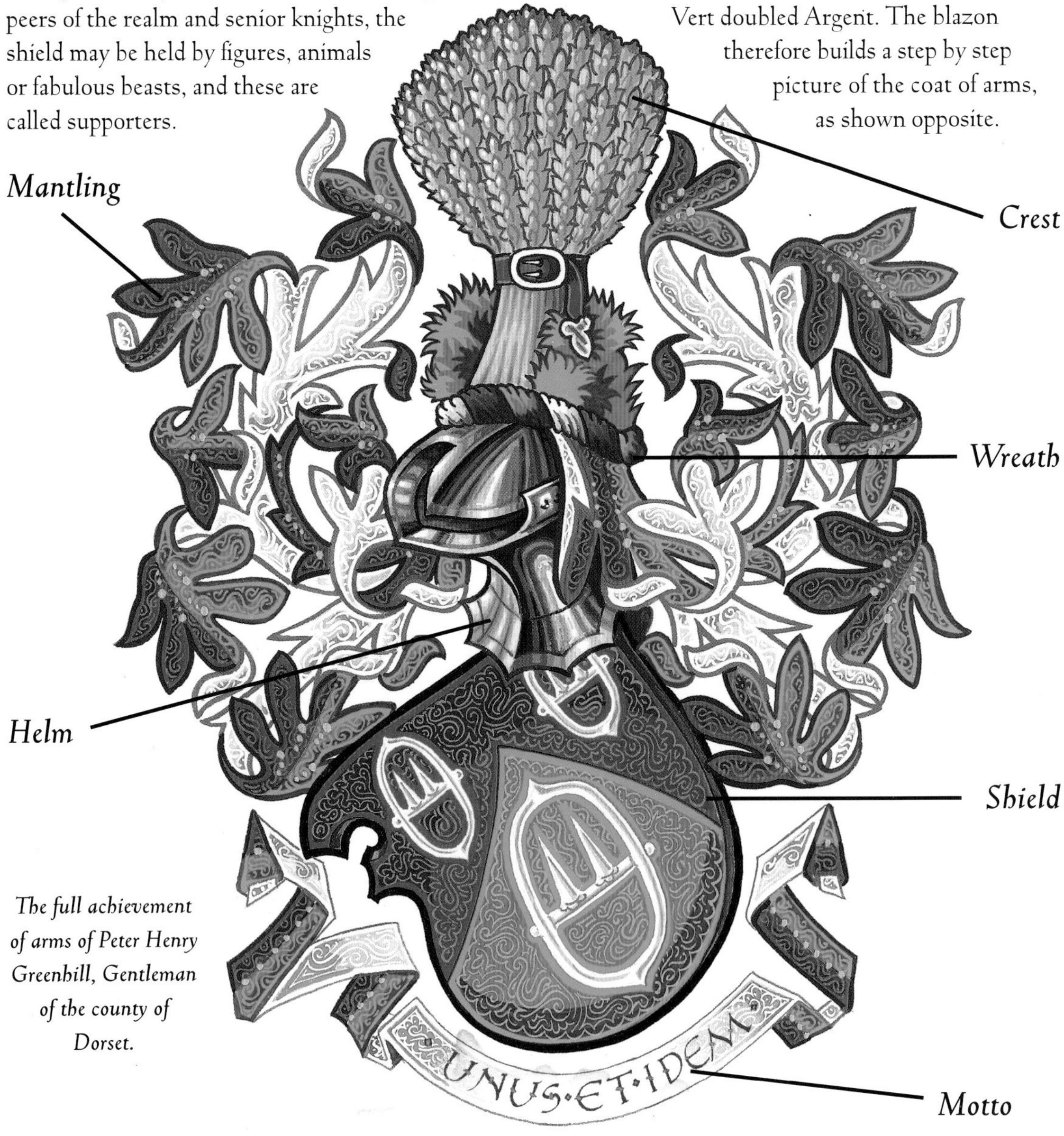

Crest

Mantling

Wreath

Helm

Shield

The full achievement of arms of Peter Henry Greenhill, Gentleman of the county of Dorset.

UNUS·ET·IDEM

Motto

12

· the shield of arms ·

Per chevron

Gules and Vert

three oval Buckles two and one their double tongues upward Argent

· the crest ·

upon a Helm

with a Wreath, Argent, Gules and Vert

between two Grassy Hillocks proper

a Garb Or

banded of a Strap Gules garnished with a buckle double tongued Argent Mantled Gules and Vert doubled Argent

The Lion and the Unicorn

The Royal Arms ➔ of Her Majesty Queen Elizabeth II, quartering the arms of England, Scotland and Ireland.

↑ The Royal Arms of England.

THE ROYAL ARMS used today by Her Majesty Queen Elizabeth II have evolved over nine centuries.

The Royal Arms of England (Gules, three Lions Passant Guardant Or) were first used by Richard the Lionheart and remained in use on their own until 1340 when King Edward III 'quartered' them with the Ancient Royal Arms of France (a blue shield Semé de lis) to symbolize his claim to the French throne. Henry IV changed the French quarter to show only three fleur-de-lis, known as 'France Modern', and they remained in this form until the reign of James I, who quartered them with the arms of Scotland and the harp of Ireland. The Hanovarian monarchs, who followed the house of Stuart, included in their arms heraldic references to their German possessions, including the famous white horse of Hanover. Queen Victoria adopted a simplified form of the Royal Arms which remain unchanged to this day.

The supporters to the Royal Arms have undergone many changes and have numbered falcons, yales, white lions, white boars, greyhounds, red dragons and, of course, the unicorn amongst their esteemed ranks.

The crown is the symbol of monarchy and sovereignty and as such has appeared in various styles in royal heraldry. It was not until the reign of Charles II that we see the heraldic crown we are familiar with today. It is based on St Edward's Crown.

↑ *The Royal Arms of James 1.*

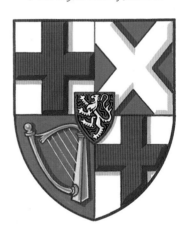

↗ *The arms of Oliver Cromwell, as Lord Protector of England, Scotland and Ireland, taken from his Great Seal.*

← *Detail from a 15th-century manuscript showing the Royal Arms of France Modern quartered with England, as used by all monarchs from Henry IV through to James I.*

St Edward's Crown, the crown used for coronations. ↘

Beasts & plants

EVERYWHERE IN HERALDRY you will find fabulous beasts. Unicorns, griffins and dragons are very familiar, but the yale, salamander and jungfraunadler (young-woman-eagle) shown here are much less common.

They all appear on coats of arms and as personal badges through the Middle Ages. In some cases, these fabulous creatures are limited only by the imaginations of medieval, Tudor and contemporary heralds.

From Richard I onwards, beasts were very popular with royalty and, by the 15th century, heralds had amassed a record of all these creatures, which have become known as the Royal Beasts. There are some superb sets of these beasts carved in stone: the King's Beasts at Hampton Court Palace, the Queen's Beasts at Kew Gardens (devised to celebrate the coronation of Elizabeth II) and the Windsor Beasts at St George's Chapel, Windsor.

Yale

Jungfraunadler

Salamander

← *These beautiful heraldic beasts are two of those to be found along the roof of St George's Chapel, Windsor, which represent the badges and supporters of many of the medieval monarchs.*

· THE LILY AND THE ROSE ·

All kinds of flowers, trees and plants have been used in heraldry – daisies, oak leaves, acorns, thistles and wheat to name but a few – but pride of place must be given to the lily and the rose. The fleur-de-lis is derived from the lily. It is very stylized on the Royal Arms of France, but appears in a more natural form on the arms of Eton College. The rose is most famously represented as the combined red and white rose of Henry VII and is still the royal badge for England.

Tudor rose

Fleur-de-lis

Peers of the Realm

A baron's coronet. ↘

PEERS OF THE REALM (more commonly known as the Lords) use a coronet in various styles above the shield to denote his or her rank. An earl has a coronet that shows five pearls and four gold strawberry leaves. A viscount's coronet shows nine pearls and a baron's shows four pearls. In addition all peers are entitled to a Helm of Degree, which is a tournament helmet in silver with gold bars. Peers of the realm are also entitled to supporters.

The Duke of Norfolk holds the hereditary office of Earl Marshal of England. His coat of arms shows his coronet of rank above his shield and his insignia of office – two gold batons with black enamel tips crossed in saltire – behind his shield. The circlet of the Order of the Garter appears around the shield.

SOLA VIRTUS INVICTA

↖ *The arms of the Duke of Norfolk.*

18

Garters, fleeces & thistles

THE SECULAR ORDERS of knighthood were quite different to those religious orders founded to fight in the Crusades. Mostly founded by sovereigns, they were used as an ultimate reward for services to the crown or royal household.

Some orders were founded on a chivalric ideal. The most famous were the Order of the Garter founded by King Edward III and the Order of the Golden Fleece founded by Philip the Bold, Duke of Burgundy.

Each order usually had a King of Arms who was responsible for recording the arms of its members. The arms were, as in the case of the Golden Fleece, often beautifully painted in a book. Those of the Garter were superbly enamelled on stall-plates in St George's Chapel, Windsor, and are one of the finest collections of heraldic art.

The United Kingdom has many orders of knighthood including the Order of the Thistle, the Order of St Michael and St George and the Order of the Bath. All members of these orders may display their medals and insignia as part of their coat of arms.

↗ *The stall-plate of Richard Beauchamp, Earl of Warwick, Knight of the Garter is enamelled on copper.*

← *Her Majesty The Queen, HRH The Duke of Edinburgh and HRH The Prince of Wales wearing the robes and insignia of the Most Ancient and Noble Order of the Thistle.*

Church heraldry

THE CHURCH ADOPTED heraldic devices both for practical identification, and, by featuring objects of devotion, to reflect and glorify God.

Amongst the most common symbols found on ecclesiastical heraldry are the keys of St Peter, crosiers, mitres, crowns, references to saints, representations of the four evangelists, the eagle of St John and so forth, and, of course, an infinite variety of crosses.

Church of England clergy may use their own coats of arms, but recently more appropriate insignia have been assigned to them to reflect their religious status. Archbishops and bishops display a mitre, and other clergy now display various forms of ecclesiastical hat which have different coloured cords and tassels attached, according to seniority within the Church.

↗ The arms of Dr George Carey, the Archbishop of Canterbury, show his personal arms on the sinister impaled with his arms of office on the dexter. His insignia of office (a mitre and two crosiers) are placed on and in saltire behind his shield.

The recently granted arms of a Catholic →
Benedictine priest, Dom Thomas Regan O.S.B.

A dean, for example, can use a black hat with two purple cords and three red tassels attached to each cord.

Members of the Roman Catholic Church do not come under the jurisdiction of the officers of arms, but the insignia they use are regulated according to a warrant issued in 1967. For example, a Catholic archbishop's arms may include a green hat with two green cords and ten green tassels on each cord, and he may also place a double traversed cross behind his shield.

The arms of His Holiness Pope John Paul II. Above ↗ the shield is the triple tiara, emblem of the papacy, and behind the shield the 'crossed' keys of St Peter. The shield of arms represents Mary at the foot of the Cross.

↘ *The arms of Cardinal Wolsey, who died in 1530, are now used by Christ Church, Oxford, and are based on a carving in Hampton Court Palace.*

LIONS OF SCOTLAND

↑ *The Royal Arms as used in Scotland, with the Scottish quarterings taking precedence.*

THE UNITED KINGDOM of Great Britain and Northern Ireland is divided into three heraldic jurisdictions: Scotland, controlled by Lord Lyon, King of Arms, and the officers of arms beneath him; Northern Ireland, which comes under the control of Norroy and Ulster King of Arms; and England, which includes Wales.

In Scotland only the heir may inherit the arms of the father. The heir may be male, female or heir of tailzie (one nominated within a blood relationship). Lord Lyon is also enacted to choose the rightful heir to a clan or

The arms of Mary Queen of Scots, from → her chambers at the Palace of Holyroodhouse in Edinburgh.

family name. In Scotland, where the clan system is all important, the arms with suitable differences are used by the chief's family and near relatives, while other members of the clan may wear a badge – usually the chief's crest surrounded by a strap and buckle bearing a motto.

Many of the clan chiefs have supporters to their arms, whereas in England few people other than peers of the realm are permitted to have them.

↑ Guidon of Peter Drummond-Murray of Mastrick showing his puffin badge, marking the fact that his mother's family owned Lundy, which in Norse means 'Isle of Puffins'.

↙ The arms of Peter Drummond-Murray of Mastrick, Slains Pursuivant of Arms to the Earl of Erroll, Lord High Constable of Scotland. (The slains pursuivant is the personal herald to the Earl of Erroll.)

↓ The shield of Sir James Douglas. The heart refers to a promise made by Douglas to the dying Robert the Bruce, to take the Bruce's heart to the Holy Land.

23

Dragons & harps

↗ *The arms of Llewellyn, Prince of Wales, who died in 1240. These arms form part of the current arms of HRH The Prince of Wales.*

↗ *The arms of Bleddyn ap Maenarch, who was descended from King Caradog Freichfras.*

↑ *The arms of O'Connor.*

MANY HISTORICAL ARMS in Wales were devised for people who lived (and some for people who had not even existed) before the advent of heraldry. It was assumed that royal and tribal ancestors were entitled to bear arms, and that their descendants were entitled to the same arms! In the 15th and 16th centuries, heralds were appointed to bring some order to the proceedings.

Today Welsh armorial matters are dealt with by the College of Arms in London. In 1963 a Wales Herald Extraordinary was appointed for the first time since the 14th century.

Heraldic practice in Northern Ireland differs little from England: the arms descend to all male descendants and the right to bear arms must be established by proof of legitimate descent from an ancestor who had arms granted. The King of Arms can issue a confirmation of arms so long as the recipient can prove that at least three generations bore the arms before 1800.

In the Republic of Ireland, the Chief Herald is responsible for all heraldic matters, granting and confirming arms to persons of Irish descent all over the world.

In Wales, the charges used often refer to some heroic deed as recounted by the bards, whilst, in the Republic of Ireland, Catholic families often include charges of a religious nature, for example, a hand holding a crucifix.

Cities & councils

↓ *The arms of the City of London date from the middle of the 14th century and combine the cross of St George and the sword of St Paul – though this is popularly thought to be the dagger used by Lord Mayor Walworth to kill Wat Tyler, the leader of the Peasants' Revolt, in 1381!*

↓ *The arms of the City of London's most famous Lord Mayor – the merchant, Dick Whittington.*

IN THE MIDDLE AGES cities and towns adapted their seals to create shields of arms reflecting royal or noble patronage. By the 16th century the heralds were granting arms in their own right to cities, towns and corporations. The city of Bristol, for example, had its arms recorded in 1623.

New arms are still created every year, as councillors realize that the whole history of their area can be reflected in a coat of arms that will last for centuries.

The arms of ↗ West Dorset District Council.

SERVICE WITH HONOUR

Guilds & Institutions

↗ The arms of the Worshipful Company of Salters of the City of London.

↗ The arms of the Worshipful Company of Scriveners of the City of London.

Heraldry is often used on pub → signs. This pub sign in the Cotswolds shows the arms of the Worshipful Company of Clothiers. The other shows the arms of the head of the Cavendish family, the Duke of Devonshire.

IN THE MIDDLE AGES, craftsmen in the cities formed guilds to protect their craft and to ensure control of the market place. On civic occasions members of each guild or company would wear the livery of their company, and so in the City of London on a great occasion you would find the Butchers' Company wearing white and blue, the Bakers' in olive green and maroon and the Wax Chandlers' also in blue and white.

The arms of the company would reflect the craft they were associated with. Painters, for example, usually had white shields, alluding to the fact that they were waiting to be painted! The Skinners' Company of the City of London was allowed to use ermine, although under medieval sumptuary law it was normally reserved for royalty and nobility as a mark of their exclusiveness and importance.

Schools and universities have also used coats of arms over the centuries. For universities the arms recorded or granted were based on those of the college founders as, for example, those of Christ's College, Cambridge, founded by Lady Margaret Beaufort. Eton College was granted arms by its founder Henry VI in 1449, and the lilies in its arms represent the Virgin Mary, to whom the College is dedicated.

Other public institutions, such as the BBC, use coats of arms, as do learned societies, such as the Heraldry Society and the Royal Society. More recently, commercial companies have received grants of arms, for example, Aquascutum of London and Harrods. Many private and commercial companies and institutions have realized that a coat of arms imparts a sense of dignity and timelessness. Heraldry is a thriving tradition that, as we head into the 21st century, is ready to adapt to the future while retaining a firm and noble link with the past.

↗ The arms of Eton College.   ↗ The arms of the Heraldry Society.

↑ Badge devised by the author for the Fellowship of the White Shield, an exclusive society for heraldic artists founded in Ottawa, Canada, in 1996. The badge represents heraldic artists from all points of the globe bound together by friendship (gold rope) and their art (white shield).

The arms ↗ recently granted to Harrods Ltd.

↗ The arms of Aquascutum of London. The white Chief and rain drops represent a cloud burst, whilst the crown shows royal patronage.

27

The Right to Arms

WHO IS ENTITLED to bear arms? The answer is simple – almost everyone. In Britain and other countries that have an heraldic authority you must petition the Earl Marshall through the necessary officers of arms for a grant of armorial bearings. Once accepted as a suitable candidate for arms, and the fee paid, you will be assigned arms.

First a sketch will be drawn of the proposed arms. Once the sketch has been signed by the petitioner, he can begin to use them. As he may not see his illuminated vellum document for anything up to three years, the Fellowship of the White Shield (see address opposite) can help him obtain the services of a professional heraldic artist, who will advise him on the design of armorial letterheads, bookplates, banners and the full range of heraldic accessories.

The arms of Dr Paul Nutley, →
devised by the author
and granted by
HM College of Arms.

← The arms of
Stephen Screech
granted by
H M College of Arms.

In countries that do not have any heraldic authority, an individual should contact a professional heraldist or artist who can devise, for a fee, a suitable coat of arms for the client.

You can find out if you are permitted to use an existing coat of arms by tracing your father's family tree. The National Register is a record of birth, marriage and death certificates for about the last 150 years. Each certificate provides a set of clues to help you search further. A birth certificate gives the name of the child's parents, and a death certificate gives the deceased's date of birth. Look, too, for information in the census records and parish registers for the districts where your ancestors lived.

A NOTE OF WARNING!

There are companies that specialize in selling coats of arms of family names. These companies should be avoided at all costs. The coat of arms assigned to you will be the first one they can find associated with your surname. Unless you can prove direct descent in the male line from the original bearer, you are not permitted by the Law of Arms to use any such arms.

• CADENCY •

As each son in England may bear his father's arms, cadency marks are used to denote each son in the family. The eldest displays a label, the second son a crescent, the third a molet and the fourth a martlet, and so on until the ninth! A daughter may now use her father's arms, or her own arms, on a shield, with the cadency mark of a small shield, in chief.

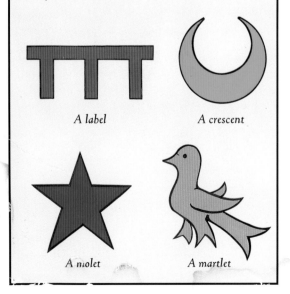

A label *A crescent*

A molet *A martlet*